MW00395954

A Daughter's Grief Journal

A Daughter's Grief Journal

Daily Prompts and Exercises
for Navigating the Loss of Your Mother

DIANE P. BRENNAN

ROCKRIDGE
PRESS

Copyright © 2021 by Rockridge Press, Emeryville, California

No part of this publication may be reproduced, stored in a retrieval system, or transmitted in any form or by any means, electronic, mechanical, photocopying, recording, scanning, or otherwise, except as permitted under Sections 107 or 108 of the 1976 United States Copyright Act, without the prior written permission of the Publisher. Requests to the Publisher for permission should be addressed to the Permissions Department, Rockridge Press, 6005 Shellmound Street, Suite 175, Emeryville, CA 94608.

Limit of Liability/Disclaimer of Warranty: The Publisher and the author make no representations or warranties with respect to the accuracy or completeness of the contents of this work and specifically disclaim all warranties, including without limitation warranties of fitness for a particular purpose. No warranty may be created or extended by sales or promotional materials. The advice and strategies contained herein may not be suitable for every situation. This work is sold with the understanding that the Publisher is not engaged in rendering medical, legal, or other professional advice or services. If professional assistance is required, the services of a competent professional person should be sought. Neither the Publisher nor the author shall be liable for damages arising herefrom. The fact that an individual, organization, or website is referred to in this work as a citation and/or potential source of further information does not mean that the author or the Publisher endorses the information the individual, organization, or website may provide or recommendations they/it may make.

Further, readers should be aware that websites listed in this work may have changed or disappeared between when this work was written and when it is read.

For general information on our other products and services or to obtain technical support, please contact our Customer Care Department within the United States at (866) 744-2665, or outside the United States at (510) 253-0500.

Rockridge Press publishes its books in a variety of electronic and print formats. Some content that appears in print may not be available in electronic books, and vice versa.

TRADEMARKS: Rockridge Press and the Rockridge Press logo are trademarks or registered trademarks of Callisto Media Inc. and/or its affiliates, in the United States and other countries, and may not be used without written permission. All other trademarks are the property of their respective owners. Rockridge Press is not associated with any product or vendor mentioned in this book.

Interior and Cover Designer: Amanda Kirk
Art Producer: Megan Baggott
Editor: Carolyn Abate
Production Editor: Mia Moran
Production Manager: Michael Kay

Author photo courtesy of Jessa Anderson Photography.

Paperback ISBN: 978-1-63807-058-0
eBook ISBN: 978-1-63807-725-1
R0

This Journal Belongs to

_____

Contents

Introduction viii

How to Use This Journal x

1 Reacting to
Your Loss 1

2 Coping with
Your Loss 29

3 Processing
Uncomfortable
Feelings 57

4 Keeping Your
Connection
Alive 83

5 Using Gratitude
to Grieve 109

6 Moving On
Without
Letting Go 133

Resources 156   **References 157**

Introduction

I am glad you are here and chose this journal. You have experienced a major loss and are grieving, a universal human experience that everyone will face and work through at some point in their lives. Having visited the depths of grief myself, I understand exactly where you are.

I experienced the loss of three family members in a short period of time. Although my losses may be different from yours, grief is grief. Grief can feel like a huge tidal wave that knocks you down and takes your breath away. It can be debilitating at times. I experienced emotional highs and lows, crying, anger, disbelief that this could be happening, and wondered if my family could survive the loss of these three people.

Well, we did survive. The first couple of years were the most challenging. I was sad, I was angry, my body hurt, and I withdrew socially. I felt that life was so unfair. In time, my grief shifted and changed. My anger eased and I became more social. As a family, we were managing through all the changes and life continued forward as we adjusted to the new dynamics and family roles.

Now, more than 20 years later, I see my grief in a different way. I know that I grew as a person and learned about myself through my struggles with grief. Although the pain was unbearable at times and life was very different, I survived and thrived. Emotionally, I am stronger and more capable of handling my feelings and emotions.

Grief has a different place in my life. I chose to become a grief counselor, to work with people who are in the throes of grief and working through the life changes that happen after a loss. This has been the most rewarding path for me, to be able to give back to others with the knowledge and under-standing of what they are going through.

This journal was created intentionally for daughters who are grieving the death of their mother, regardless of the relationship they shared. Whether your relationship was challenging or filled with beautiful moments, this journal will help you connect with your innermost thoughts and feelings. It will be a safe space for you to reflect on this loss, process your feelings, and begin to heal. We will work through your feelings and experiences right after your loss, coping with and processing your feelings, finding ways to keep your connec-tions alive, feeling grateful, and then restoring balance and moving on.

Healing takes time and patience. Your mom may have suffered from a long illness, died suddenly as a result of an accident, or passed away unex-pectedly due to a medical condition. The fact is, your mom has died and it feels awful. Our mothers symbolize life; she gave birth to you and that is what is most unique to this loss. In addition, our mothers have a significant role in nurturing us and helping us grow from children into adults. This loss deeply connects to how you relate to the world as a daughter.

Use this journal as a guide to assist you in navigating your grief. Be gentle with yourself as you grieve. You will get through this and heal. This I know to be true.

How to Use
This Journal

There is no right or wrong way to grieve. The process that you will go through is highly personal and unique to you. That is why you should approach using this book in a way that works best for you. There are six sections. As you begin to write, go where you feel the strongest pull. For example, if you are struggling with difficult emotions like anger, resentment, and guilt, start with section 3, Processing Uncomfortable Feelings. You may also want to begin with section 5, Using Gratitude to Grieve. Many of the contemporary models of grief suggest that when we grieve, it is important to continue our relationship with the deceased, building a continuous and lasting bond.

This journal includes reflections, writing prompts, and exercises that will assist you in working through your feelings of grief. Grief doesn't have a timeline, so do not feel rushed to get through the journal; go at your own pace. Focus on what is meaningful and most useful to you. Make this journal your own. I do recommend making a commitment to journaling on a regular basis, whether that means one entry each day, every other day, or once a week. Try to be consistent with your writing as you work through the journal. It is meant to support and guide you as you grieve, so use it as such.

Many contemporary theories of grief discuss the importance of working through the pain of the loss and adjusting to the world without the deceased. This means confronting feelings of sadness, anger, guilt, and denial. Researchers Klass, Silverman, and Nickman explain the significance of remaining connected to the deceased in their Continuing Bonds theory. They found that continuing a relationship with the deceased provides both support and comfort as we grieve. It is normal to want to remain connected to your mom and actually helps you cope with the loss. It's important to note that grief can be challenging and difficult. You may need to seek professional help if you are experiencing symptoms related to depression, anxiety, or trauma. This journal is not a substitute for professional treatment.

As you work on integrating this loss into your life, be patient with yourself and others around you. The path to healing is not a straight line. You will have to navigate through the twists and turns of grief as you find your way forward. Take your time. Go at your own pace. Nurture yourself as you heal.

"I do know that mother loss can be heartbreaking at any age. No matter how old we are, we yearn for a mother's love throughout our lives, reaching for the security and comfort we believe only she can provide at times of illness, transition, or stress."

— HOPE EDELMAN, *MOTHERLESS DAUGHTERS: THE LEGACY OF LOSS*

1
REACTING TO YOUR LOSS

———

No matter what your relationship was like, losing your mother can result in deep pain when the bonds to this significant figure in life are cut. It is through our grieving process that we learn how to adjust to the world without our mom. There is no set timeline for how long our grief will last and no way to predict how we will react to the loss of our mother. Grief shows up in different ways through feelings of anger, regret, sadness, and even joy. So, it's important to take the time to acknowledge your loss, understand your grief reactions, and accept that you are grieving. This first section provides a framework to explore your initial grief reactions following the loss of your mother.

The one thing you might notice early on in your grieving process is that you have difficulty controlling it. You can't place grief in a nice, neat, linear timeline. One day it comes on strong, the next day it's nearly absent. As you open yourself up to grieving, you begin to acknowledge the uncertainty of your days and learn how to make room for grief in your life. Begin each day knowing that you will welcome grief into your daily routine, however it shows up.

Acknowledging Your Feelings

In grief, we experience a broad range of feelings; some are familiar while others are new and different. Understanding the full range of feelings is helpful in creating a path toward healing. This exercise will help you identify and acknowledge the grief-related feelings that are present right now.

1. In the space below, draw a circle and write "Mom" in the center.

2. Think about your feelings related to your mom before her death. List them on the left side of the circle.

3. Think about your feelings related to your mom after her death. List them on the right side of the circle.

4. Look at the feelings you listed and note what is the same prior to and after her death.

5. Circle the feelings that are most intense right now.

6. Select three feelings and commit to working with them.

▶▶▶ **Comprehending the loss of your mom is not easy.** Disbelief and even denial may dominate your thoughts. Confront your disbelief by replacing those thoughts with confirming statements. Doing so helps with accepting the reality that the loss happened. For example: "This is not a dream. It is real and I will find a way to heal." Write a few statements to confront your disbelief.

▶▶▶ **No matter how well you prepare for the inevitable day, the loss of your mother will come as a shock.** That feeling can last for a while. However, there are steps you can take to ease into your grief. Acknowledging how your world has changed since her death is a start. What has changed for you now that your mother is no longer here? Write about what comes to mind; spare no details.

▶▶▶**Getting used to grief requires both time and energy.** Slowing down allows for healing and reflection. Take a look at your schedule and challenge yourself to lighten your load. Plan for quiet time, get a massage, or take a long walk. What are some ways you can shift into low gear to make room for grieving?

No two people experience the same grief reactions. Shortly following the death of your mother, you may experience intense feelings of shock, numbness, anger, guilt, or sadness. You may experience mental effects such as confusion, forgetfulness, or difficulty making decisions. Socially, you may withdraw or avoid certain events or situations. You may feel fatigued, or have unexplained pain or sleep disruptions. You may notice changes in your spiritual practices. These are all normal grief reactions.

Labeling Your Emotions

It can be challenging to express your feelings of grief. Sometimes the words won't come, while other times there won't be enough. Uncovering your feelings through a visual representation of your grief can create a connection to your deepest emotions.

1. Begin with a look through your own photographs or visit a favorite website that has images you can view online. You can also flip through a magazine.

2. As you look through the pictures and photographs, notice what reactions arise and how they relate to your feelings of grief.

3. Once you have selected three to five pictures, return to this journal and use the space provided to make notes about your feelings of grief that are reflected in the pictures.

▶▶▶ **It's expected that you will feel sadness in the mix of all your feelings following the loss of your mom.** You may feel sad that she cannot be a grandmother to your children or give you advice. Perhaps your relationship was strained at the time of her death and that makes you feel all sorts of emotions. We feel our sadness in many ways. What makes you feel saddest about your mother's death?

▶▶▶ **The loss of a mother causes many people to think about missed opportunities.** In other words, as you grieve, you'll likely find yourself reflecting on what you could have done, should have done, or might have done at different times during your mom's life. These unsettled feelings are about guilt and are very common among people who are grieving. What's more, it can be hard to reconcile feelings of guilt and offer forgiveness to yourself. What feelings of guilt are you holding around the death of your mother?

▶▶▶ **It's a perfectly understandable to feel angry when reacting to the loss of your mother.** Anger is a strong feeling we can have following a painful or bad experience. Anger can be diffused by intentionally shifting our focus away from it and moving toward calming behaviors. What activities can you engage in to bring your body and mind into an overall state of calm and relaxation?

Finding Balance with Grief

In the early days, weeks, and months of grief, you may not feel like doing anything. But the reality is that life doesn't stop—even in your darkest days. Finding balance between confronting grief and engaging in life's daily activities is key. This visualization exercise will help you regulate your emotions and find a balance between confronting your grief and focusing on important tasks. Plan to use this exercise at a time when you need to set your grief aside in order to focus on completing an important activity or task.

1. Construct a container using your imagination.

2. What shape is the container: round, square, rectangle? What color is it?

3. Hold a visual of the container in your mind.

4. Open the container and place all of your grief inside. Close the container.

5. Imagine placing the container in a safe place. You can put it on a shelf in a closet or under your bed, knowing that you can retrieve the container at any time.

6. Acknowledge that your feelings of grief are in the container and you will be able to take them out of the container later.

7. Turn your focus to completing the activities that require your attention.

8. Return to the safe place that you imagined earlier and retrieve the container.

9. Open the container and reengage with your grief.

▶▶▶ **In the weeks and months following the loss of your mom, it can feel like a fog has descended over you.** Making decisions can be difficult, and remembering the simplest things can be challenging. Focus on lightening your load and ask others for help in completing tasks. What tasks can others assist you with right now? Make a list.

▶▶▶ **It's natural to experience fear as part of grief.** Fear stems from uncertainty and not feeling secure. You might become fearful of your emotions and not being able to control them, or fearful of what might happen in the future. You can also be fearful of not grieving the right way. What are the fears associated with the loss of your mother that you are feeling right now?

▶▶▶ **As mentioned before, grief doesn't map out its plan complete with warning signs when twists and turns are coming.** In fact, you will be surprised by your grief at the most inopportune or unusual times. Grief can ambush you while you're in the grocery store, watching a TV show, or out dining with friends. In what ways have you been ambushed by your grief?

You might be wondering how long your grief will last. The truth is, you will experience grief over the death of your mom throughout your life. Your grief is going to shift and change over time, moving from an all-consuming feeling in your early grief to a more manageable, occasional feeling of grief. As we learn more about our grief and how to interact with it, it will become less noticeable—and less painful—in our daily lives.

▶▶▶ **When your mother dies, you will likely be confronted with many realizations—one being that there isn't anything you can do to prevent the death of someone you love.** Learning to acknowledge that you are powerless over death can shift your focus away from feeling helpless. Doing so can bring your attention to living a meaningful life. In what ways can you honor your mom by living a life filled with purpose and meaning?

▶▶▶ **There will be times when it seems like there is nothing that can be done to control or stop your heartache and sorrow.** Perhaps you've already experienced this? Talking with others along with nurturing and caring for yourself are important when tending to your broken heart. What can you do to soothe your broken heart?

Your Changing Worldview

Loss changes the way we see the world and how we interact within it. When your worldview changes because of a loss, that new reality may prove to be more challenging. You may find yourself clinging to your pre-loss life. Even if you and your mother weren't on great terms at the time of her death or you never had a close relationship with her, this feeling will still hold true. This exercise provides you with an opportunity to work on defining new expectations for your post-loss world. Complete this statement and list as many items as you can:

▶▶▶ Things might feel different in my life as I grieve the loss of my mother, but I can find new ways to . . .

_____

_____

_____

_____

_____

_____

_____

_____

▶▶▶ **To be happy while you're mourning the loss of your mother can feel strange, because it's two opposing forces pushing for your attention.** Feeling guilty for being happy comes with knowing that your mom will never be able to share in your joy. One way to release your guilt is to recall a time when your mom was happy for you and write about that experience.

_____

_____

_____

_____

_____

_____

_____

_____

_____

_____

_____

_____

_____

▶▶▶ **Grief has been described as overwhelming and all consuming.** What would be helpful for you when the pain of the loss consumes you and feels so overwhelming?

Drawing Upon Resilience

Being resilient in grief means that we intentionally focus our thoughts on the positive, reminding ourselves of the good that exists in our life. Purposefully drawing upon positive memories of your mom to keep the memories alive can help. Look for opportunities to grow as an individual because of this loss, choosing to put your attention on the nourishing or loving aspects of your relationships and not on the difficult ones.

Take a few minutes and reflect on the following questions: What approaches have you used in the past to cope with and overcome challenges? What insights can you draw upon from past losses that apply now? What resilient behaviors can you use to help move through your grief?

Imagine that you are traveling through the jungle and come across a patch of quicksand. Your instinct will be to avoid the quicksand and navigate around it. We need to do the same thing with grief and navigate around it at times to avoid sinking further into it. Think about who or what pulls you out of the quicksand of your grief. Keep this in mind for the next time you find yourself sinking into the depths of your grief.

▶▶▶ **It's important to reach out to others when we are feeling lonely or overwhelmed by grief.** Who are the people that have been most helpful as you adapt to living in a world without your mom? Write their names and how their support has contributed to easing your grief.

_____

_____

_____

_____

_____

_____

_____

_____

"Deep grief sometimes is almost like a specific location, a coordinate on a map of time. When you are standing in that forest of sorrow, you cannot imagine that you could ever find your way to a better place. But if someone can assure you that they themselves have stood in that same place, and now have moved on, sometimes this will bring hope." —ELIZABETH GILBERT, *EAT, PRAY, LOVE*

"There is no way around the pain
you feel when someone you love dies.
You can go over it, under it or around it...
Going through it is what helps you heal."

— THERESE RANDO, *HOW TO GO ON LIVING WHEN
SOMEONE YOU LOVE DIES*

2
COPING WITH YOUR LOSS

———

Grieving is hard work. Coping with the demands of daily life following the loss of your mother is challenging. Each day requires a shift between your grief and life's other responsibilities. This switching back and forth makes it tough to find your footing and bring your life back into balance. There are times when you can feel like a fundamentally different person and are unsure of what can be done to ease your grief. When you are in deep grief, it is necessary to take care of yourself first in order to navigate the daily demands of your life. This section helps you examine your current coping strategies and identify new ways to put yourself first while grieving.

Sadness, anger, fear, guilt, regret, joy, and hope are just a few examples of feelings we may encounter when grieving. Our emotions can get trapped inside of us and they need an outlet. Finding ways to cope with the emotional pain of losing your mother is an essential part of grieving. Even if your relationship with your mom wasn't ideal, it's important to grieve the loss. Giving yourself the green light to fully experience the messiness of your grief is both freeing and essential to working through your pain.

Releasing Emotions through Letter Writing

Writing is a healthy and productive way to cope with feelings of grief. It allows you to continue your relationship with the person who died, or even to begin a new one. Continuing your relationship or constructing a new meaningful connection with your mom is important because even though she is not here anymore, you may still want to lean on her. That is what writing can offer you. For this exercise, set aside 30 minutes and find a comfortable space. You will be writing two letters.

▶▶▶ **The first letter will be from you to your mom.** You may choose to tell her what has been going on in your life or something that you wish you had told her before she died. The most important thing is to allow yourself to express what you are feeling inside.

▶▶▶**The second letter will be a letter to you from your mom.** In this letter, your mom can tell you how much she misses you or give you advice or words of comfort to help ease your grief. Use your imagination to create the dialogue and write from the perspective of your mother.

▶▶▶ **We often don't think about the connection between our mind and body, but our thoughts and feelings have an impact on how we feel physically.** People in grief will describe feeling physically drained and talk about body aches. Knowing that grief can exist in our bodies, it's important to routinely engage in physical activity. This can be as simple as taking a walk or going for a bike ride. What ways would you like to move your body to help it release some of your grief?

▶▶▶ **Making the right choices about nutrition can be overwhelming when we are deep in grief.** Eating proper meals can easily get pushed to the wayside. But ensuring that your body has the proper nourishment while grieving is essential to your healing process. Implementing a simple routine for eating can help you eat well. Commit to eating three meals a day at set times, whether or not you are hungry, to sustain you. Write down your meal schedule for the next week.

▶▶▶ **Objects that belonged to your mom are able to provide comfort in grief.**
These direct emotional connections are called linking objects. Some examples
of linking objects include a piece of jewelry, a purse or wallet, a recipe, or a
piece of clothing. Make a list of five items belonging to your mom that can be
used during difficult moments to help ease your grief.

One of the hardest things to understand about grief is that everyone's experience is different. A lot of one's experience depends on personality, life situation, and the relationship with the person who died. People wonder if they are grieving in the right way or in a healthy manner. To answer that question, think about your coping strategies. You may likely seek support and comfort from others and actively process feelings of grief. You may also realize and accept that making mistakes and being confused is part of grieving. You may begin to identify ways to remain connected to your mom, acknowledge the reality of the loss, and engage in building a positive outlook for the future. These are all positive coping strategies that are strongly encouraged for you to explore and engage.

Preserving Your Memories

Creating a safe place for storing memories and remembrances of your mother can have a positive influence on grief. Collecting these items helps process your feelings and reduce worry about forgetting her in the future. This exercise will guide you through creating a memory box to hold special keepsakes and objects that have deep personal meaning.

1. Purchase a decorative box or create one yourself. You might want the box to reflect your mom's favorite color or sparkle because it makes you feel joyful. Whatever you choose should remind you of your mother.

2. Gather items that you will want to place in the box. You should include sentimental trinkets, cards, or letters that your mom wrote to you. Maybe there is a photo that you treasure, a small sampling of the perfume she wore, or something from the funeral or a condolence card that someone sent to you.

3. Place each item in the box and reflect on the memory connected to the item.

4. Once you have placed all the items in the box, jot down any additional memories or feelings that you have on a piece of paper and add it to the box.

5. Store your memory box in a safe place and open it whenever you want to actively engage with your memories.

▶▶▶ **Following the loss of your mother, it is normal to wonder about death and what happens after.** Death is front and center in your life right now, and your thoughts can drift toward your beliefs about dying. Acknowledging these thoughts allows you release any anxiety and brings relief to your grieving process. What unspoken fears do you have about death and dying?

▶▶▶ **Questioning your faith and spiritual beliefs—whatever they may be—is typical following the loss of your mom.** After your mother dies, it's normal to reflect on any lessons you learned from her. To think about beliefs and traditions can bring about comfort. But you may also find yourself questioning your beliefs and challenging them. Both are okay. How does the loss of your mom fit into your religious or spiritual beliefs?

▶▶▶ **After losing your mom, you may find yourself avoiding certain situations or experiences to protect yourself from triggers of pain and sorrow.** This could include certain songs, restaurants, books, or movies. It's understandable that you want to avoid these things, but when we do that, we also avoid processing our feelings of grief. What have you been avoiding because you are afraid it will trigger painful emotions?

The ways you cope with the death of your mother can be both healthy and unhealthy. It's important to understand the unhealthy methods of coping, so you recognize them and replace them with healthier strategies. After your mother dies, it can feel like the world is out of control and everything you know to be true has changed. Your boundaries may slip, which can be revealed in overeating, not eating at all, or relying on drugs and alcohol to ease your pain. Risky behaviors, such as self-harm and unsafe sexual practices, are other unhealthy ways of coping. If you find that you are reliant on unhealthy coping strategies, it is important to seek the help of a professional counselor. They will help you reset and engage in healthy coping strategies to work through the pain of losing your mother.

▶▶▶ In the weeks and months following the loss of your mom, you will begin to see that you are capable of things that you may never have realized before. You may notice a different level of confidence when making decisions, a renewed sense of purpose in your life, or a greater ability to let go of the small stuff. What newly discovered strengths have you developed following the loss of your mother?

▶▶▶ **Grief is unpredictable. You will experience good days and bad days.**
A good day may mean that your grief feels manageable and that you could cope well throughout the day. A bad day may mean that you're not able to assert any control over your grief, as it takes over for the entire day. What can you tell yourself here about good days that can help you when a bad day rears its ugly head?

_____

_____

_____

_____

What insights can you take from the good days to help you cope with your grief on the bad days?

_____

_____

_____

_____

Creating Personal Grief Rituals

Personal grief rituals are restorative activities that invite healing and create connectedness. They help ease our grief by allowing memories to have a more positive influence.

Grief rituals allow you to celebrate your mom's life. Going to her favorite restaurant, making her favorite dessert, and volunteering with organizations she supported are a few examples of different rituals you may consider. Make a list of the activities that you can engage in to honor your mom.

You've likely heard people say to you that it's important to take care of yourself and focus on healing from your loss. That may seem selfish to you. Perhaps you feel pressure to care for others in your family before you care for yourself. Allowing time to reflect on the loss and address your deepest feelings of grief is where healing begins. Honor that life your mother gave you and put your needs first. No matter what your relationship was with your mom, whether you were close or distant, prioritizing "me" time is essential to healing your pain.

▶▶▶ **Friends are sometimes easier than family to rely on after the loss of your mother.** They are removed from the family system and can provide you with much-needed support. Which friends have been most helpful as you adapt to living in a world without your mom? Who can you rely on during difficult moments of grief? Write their names here and how they offer you support with your grief.

_____

_____

_____

_____

_____

_____

_____

_____

_____

_____

_____

_____

_____

Your Changing Family Structure

Whenever a death occurs in a family, the structure will organically reorganize. It's safe to say that this process doesn't always go smoothly. The loss of your mother to the family structure will have a ripple effect.

Without your mom, your family will naturally settle into a new pattern. That may play out in how you communicate or plan for family gatherings. Family get-togethers will also be different. In what ways do you see your family system changing?

▶▶▶ **In the weeks and months following your mom's death, you will likely encounter people who want to offer their condolences.** Depending on the day, you may end up feeling caught between wanting to talk with them about the loss of your mom and wanting to avoid talking about it. It's helpful to prepare in advance for these moments and know how you will respond to the condolence. Keep it simple and straightforward, such as, "Thank you. I appreciate you sharing your condolences with me, although the loss is too raw right now to talk about." Think about how you will want to respond to an unexpected condolence and write it below.

When in the throes of deep grief, unrealistic expectations of others can arise. You may want family members to offer help without being asked or friends to check in more often to see how you are doing. It's disappointing when our expectations are not met, but it's important to consider whether the expectations we have set are realistic. What are your expectations of others in your grief? Challenge yourself to consider if they are reasonable and practical.

Creating Your Self-Care Plan

Just as every person's grief journey is unique, the best techniques for taking care of yourself during times of grief are personal. Creating a self-care plan allows us to set goals around restoration and healing. Ideas for self-care include exercise, deep breathing, meditation, reading a book, taking a warm bath, and eating well. List four self-care practices you enjoy. Set a goal to do one a week for the next month.

1. ....

....

....

2. ....

....

....

3. ....

....

....

4. ....

....

....

▶▶▶ **As you learned earlier in this journal, actively connecting with memories helps maintain a connection to your mother.** Engaging in creative projects is a wonderful way to connect with memories. Making a photo collage, painting, or creating a playlist of music your mom enjoyed listening to can provide an opportunity to express your emotions as you work through your grief. What creative projects do you think will support your grief during this time of mourning?

▶▶▶ **The world can seem out of control when we are grieving. At these times, we need a break from our grief.** Take a break and connect with memories of a time when you felt calm and at peace. Think about a time when you felt safe, comfortable, and relaxed. Where were you? What was it like? Describe that place in detail. When feeling overwhelmed by your grief, visualize this place when you need a grief break.

_____

_____

_____

_____

_____

_____

_____

_____

"Grief is not a disorder, a disease, or a sign of weakness. It is an emotional, physical, and spiritual necessity, the price you pay for love. The only cure for grief is to grieve." —EARL A. GROLLMAN

"Initially, there is a sense of profound shock and disbelief that this could ever happen to you. Real grief often does not hit home until much later. For many it is a grief never entirely lost. Life is altered as you know it, and not a day goes past without you thinking about the one you have lost. I know that over time it is possible to learn to live with what has happened and, with the passing of years, to retain or rediscover cherished memories."

—PRINCE WILLIAM

3

PROCESSING UNCOMFORTABLE FEELINGS

Grief is disordered, chaotic, and messy, producing an abundance of emotions that are new and different. The loss of your mother is one of life's most profound experiences, and it's usually coupled with overwhelmingly difficult and complex emotions. Feelings about the death of the person who brought you to life are often complicated and challenging. In your healing, it's important to come to terms with all of these uncomfortable feelings, some which stem from the death and others that come from the relationship you had with your mom. This section will provide prompts, exercises, and reflections to help process and manage these uncomfortable feelings.

When you're grieving, your emotions and feelings and can be triggered by just about anything: people, sounds, sights, smells, or situations. A grief trigger can arouse good memories that bring joy, or unpleasant memories and emotions that you may wish to avoid. Understanding your grief triggers can help you navigate around the uncomfortable, painful memories in order to focus on the positive, healing memories. Empower yourself in grief by focusing on positive triggers and memories as part of your grief journey.

Matching Triggers with Coping Strategies

Coping strategies are the ways that we respond when grief is triggered so that we do not become overwhelmed. They can be healthy, such as joining a support group and going for long walks, or they can be unhealthy, such as using alcohol to numb the pain and overeating. The goal of this exercise is to identify healthy ways to cope with your grief.

Coping strategy due to a grief trigger:	Is it a positive or negative behavior?	An improved coping strategy:

▶▶▶ **Let's start by examining your current coping methods and identifying ways to improve them.** Begin by thinking about what you have learned so far about your grief and how well you are coping. In the first column in the table below, list the coping behaviors that you typically default to when you encounter a grief trigger. In the second column, note whether the coping behavior is positive or negative. Then in the third column, identify ways you would like to improve your coping skills.

▶▶▶ **As you look for sources of comfort from grief, you may experience intense longing for your mom in the aftermath of her loss.** Even if your relationship wasn't close, this longing can still occur. It's important to find ways to express what it is that you are missing. What do you miss the most about your mom?

▶▶▶ **When you're grieving, it's likely you'll experience a higher level of irritability, particularly with family and close friends, and even your own self.** Irritability can be diffused through compassion, particularly toward oneself, and then extended to others. Think about a recent time when you were irritable and write about it below. How do you think that experience was related to your underlying feelings of grief?

▶▶▶ **Trust is another concern that can come up as you grieve the loss of your mother.** You might experience feelings of distrust in yourself and your decisions. This can be particularly true for women who relied heavily on their mother for guidance during different milestones in life. Even if you weren't particularly close to your mother, your world can still seem off-kilter—you may not know what or whom to trust in a given moment. In what ways do you see yourself not trusting in yourself and others? What steps can you take to regain this trust?

As the reality of your mother's death starts to really set in, you may notice an increased level of worry for others or fear about things in the future. That's because long-held beliefs have been shattered; the world is different in the aftermath of loss. When you feel anxious about living in the world without your mom, your thoughts can focus on negative outcomes and hinder your ability to see anything positive. Becoming more aware of your anxious grief thoughts will help you break free from them as you take charge over the new reality you are facing.

Letting Go of Unhelpful Thoughts

This exercise will walk you through how to replace unhelpful, negative thoughts around your grief, with positive, healing thoughts.

1. Write down a negative thought about your grief. *Example: This grief is hopeless; I am never going to be happy again without my mom.*

_____

_____

_____

2. Read the thought out loud and ask yourself: What evidence do I have to support that this is true?

3. Challenge yourself to think about the possibilities. Will this be true a year from now? Five years from now? Ten years from now?

4. Reframe the thought into a positive one and write it down. *Example: Although my grief is painful right now, I know that it will not be like this forever.*

_____

_____

_____

5. Practice saying your positive thought out loud to replace the negative thoughts.

▶▶▶ **Finding constructive ways to express grief-related anger is a natural part of the healing process.** Anger can be a healthy and positive emotion when it's used to push us forward in our grief. What are you feeling most angry about now? Write down what surfaces as a way to release those feelings. You can share your grief-related anger with someone close to you to help gain perspective.

▶▶▶ **Whatever your relationship was with your mother, her death marks the end of a physical relationship.** Perhaps your mother disagreed with your career choices or didn't like your partner. Maybe you quarreled with her in the months before she died. Maybe you never thought about addressing issues that you and mother had between the two of you. But now that she's gone, you feel guilty—or worse—about typical mother-daughter turmoil. To shift your grief and begin moving forward, write down the reasons for your guilt. Ask yourself if it is realistic to feel this way. Challenge yourself to forgive the wrongs and remember what you did right.

▶▶▶ **Shame shows up in our grief when we evaluate ourselves harshly for things which we have little control over.** We may think that it was possible to alter the course of events that led to our mother's death. Other times we believe that we are not grieving in the right way. Shame gets in the way of us expressing our true feelings. How has shame influenced your grieving process?

▶▶▶ **People often experience a sense that something was left unsaid, unfinished, or unresolved in their relationship with their mom before she died.** Unfinished business often shows up as regret for what could have been said, done, or shared. Challenge yourself to find a way to resolve these thoughts and feelings. Make a list of what you consider to be unfinished and decide what you can let go.

No parent-child relationship is picture-perfect. The complex and difficult feelings we experience after the death of our mother may originate from other times in our lives. We might have resentments from childhood that have gone unspoken, tensions from our teenage years that went unresolved, and arguments that continued in adult-hood. You might have expected that there would be more time to address the issues that existed in the relationship with your mom. Learning to forgive yourself can help resolve issues that are rooted in other times. You can find healing and peace through forgiveness.

Understanding Your Body in Grief

We often think of grief as an emotional process, forgetting that grief can also have a physical component. These steps will take you through a body scan, which can help locate tension in your body and pinpoint where you are holding grief.

1. Sit in a comfortable position and close your eyes.

2. Take three breaths, inhaling and exhaling for a count of three on each breath.

3. Focus on your head and neck; notice if there you are holding any tension here. Pause. Take three breaths.

4. Move to your chest and stomach; check for tension here. Pause. Take three breaths.

5. Go to your shoulders, arms, elbows, and fingers; check for tension here. Pause. Take three breaths.

6. Move to your hips, legs, knees, and toes; check for tension here. Pause. Take three breaths.

7. Open your eyes. Reflect on the areas of your body where you noticed tension.

8. Use the space below to make note of where your body is holding grief.

▶▶▶ **In times of grief, people tend to naturally withdraw and isolate.** It can be hard to invite others into your grief world; reaching out to others for support feels useless. It is important to avoid isolation and schedule time to do things outside your home. Make a list of five things you can do to break through your isolation, such as taking a walk or volunteering to clean up a neighborhood park. Once you have written the list, make a schedule to do these activities. Try to do one thing each day from the list.

▶▶▶ **It is natural to have fears after your mom dies:** fear of the future without your mom, fear of being anxious, fear of being overcome by unexpected emotions, fear of crying in public, fear of not crying enough. What fears are you facing as you grieve the loss of your mom?

▶▶▶ **In grief, we become guarded against the possibility of feeling any more pain and hurt.** We close ourselves up and don't talk about our loss. This prevents us from fully grieving. Challenge yourself to break through your vulnerability. You can begin by being open and honest with others about what you are going through. Think about the ways you have been holding back. Using your most authentic voice, write about the death of your mom and your grief in the space below.

Reconciling Your Relationship

Human beings instinctually seek maternal love. We grieve not only the loss of what we had and shared with our mom but also what we never had or were unable to experience in our relationship. When you reconcile your feelings about the relationship you had with your mom, it promotes healing and brings peace. Follow these steps to reflect on your relationship and reconcile any problematic feelings you have related to your mom.

1. Reflect on your relationship with your mom and how it has impacted your life.

2. Give equal consideration to both the positive and negative.

3. Think about gains and outline the strengths you have developed.

4. Take time to acknowledge areas of personal growth that have come from working through the difficult and challenging moments.

5. Give yourself the gift of grace and extend that grace to your mom.

▶▶▶ **Sometimes we hide our feelings of grief, especially when we feel relief following the death of our mother.** Death does not always cause great sadness. Relief may the predominant emotion following a long period of illness and caregiving, or because our relationship was difficult or nonexistent. Death can ease our burdens, although it is often difficult to express these feelings. In what ways do you feel relief due to the death of your mother?

_____

_____

_____

_____

_____

_____

_____

_____

_____

_____

_____

_____

_____

▶▶▶ **When your mother is no longer around, it's perfectly normal if feelings of resentment bubble up.** There's a lot of different reasons for this but the most common usually stem from feeling that our siblings did not contribute enough to caring for our mom or that our friends didn't offer enough support during this emotional time. When resentment grows, it can lead to feelings of anger and damage our relationships. A good way to resolve resentments is to look at the issue objectively from a different perspective. What resentments have you been holding on to?

_____

_____

_____

_____

Now take a moment to think about your feelings of resentment from another angle, not just your perceived hurt. How can you look at them objectively to resolve them?

_____

_____

_____

_____

_____

Looking Back as You Move Forward

The soundtrack in our mind can get stuck in a continuous loop, reviewing past mistakes we made as a daughter and regrets we have about our relationship with our mom. Taking steps to truly examine those past events and shift to the present moment will provide you new perspective, which will free you from the past and assign new purpose and meaning in the present.

1. Recall a memory that you experienced with your mom; it can be a pleasant or unpleasant memory.

2. Think about how you felt at the time when the memory occurred. Write your feelings down.

3. Take three deep breaths and shift your focus to this present moment.

4. Think about how you feel now, in this present moment, as you reflect on the past memory. Write your feelings down.

5. Compare the feelings from the past to those of the present. What do you notice about them? What feelings are similar? What feelings are different? Consider how you have grown and changed over time.

6. Take three deep breaths and release your regrets and mistakes of the past.

7. Hold space in your heart and mind for this new perspective.

Past feelings	Present feelings

▶▶▶ **Let's say you're dining out in a restaurant and the host seats you next to a mother and her adult daughter having dinner and enjoying each other's company.** You may feel a bit of jealousy rise. This feeling is natural. You can no longer have that type of intimate experience with your mom or maybe you never had that. At these moments, life seems unfair. Acknowledging that we are jealous is the first step in releasing those feelings. When have you experienced jealousy related to your grief?

_____

_____

_____

_____

_____

_____

_____

_____

_____

_____

Losing your mom results in an emotional void. Even if you and your mother didn't have a close relationship, that feeling of emptiness will resonate deep in your soul. Acknowledge that these difficult feelings exist. Then focus on mothering yourself and find ways to nurture yourself. Practice self-love and bring positive healing energy into each day.

▶▶▶ **No mother-daughter relationship is without issue.** There will be past hurts and wrongs that we reflect on in grief. Forgiveness releases the painful feelings that exist within us. It begins with an acceptance that the past cannot be changed and that holding on to the past only causes pain in the present. What are the past hurts and wrongs that you can forgive? Write them here and release them.

"Time makes it easier . . . I still miss my mother every day—and it's 20 years after she died."

—PRINCE WILLIAM

"The people we most love do become
a physical part of us, ingrained in our synapses,
in the pathways where memories are created."

—MEGHAN O'ROURKE, *THE LONG GOODBYE*

4

KEEPING YOUR
CONNECTION ALIVE

———

I t's important to remember that you will always be
your mother's daughter. This does not change after
she dies. One popular theory of grief suggests that
maintaining a relationship with the deceased while moving
forward in life is an essential part of the grieving process.
In doing so, you retain your identity as a daughter while
finding ways to remember your mom. This can be challenging because people tend to rely on past reflections and
memories as a basis for their new relationship. Even so,
finding ways to keep this connection alive to honor the
memory of your mother is the work of grief. In this section,
you will use journal prompts, reflections, and exercises to
help surface positive memories of your mother as a basis
for establishing a new connection.

In grief, you can be surprised by an overwhelming feeling that your mom is nearby. People describe sensing the presence of someone who has died by feeling sudden chills or an energetic shift in their surrounding area. Although there is no concrete scientific explanation, when we feel the presence of our mom it can comfort us. Inviting these moments instead of pushing them away allows a new and different relationship to develop. Be open to welcoming your mom's loving presence. Acknowledge the new connection. Take comfort in knowing that a new relationship is forming.

Engage Your Senses to Connect

We have five basic senses: sight, sound, touch, smell, and taste. They help us navigate the world around us and are stronger when we are in grief. You can use your senses to recall memories of your mom to help ease your emotional distress. This can be incredibly soothing and comforting.

▶▶▶ **Let's start with sight.** This could be as simple as looking at pictures of your mom, watching your favorite family video, going for a walk in the neighborhood where you grew up, being out in nature, or watching a movie. Make a list of up to five different methods using your sight to remember your mother.

▶▶▶ **Sounds such as songs or your mother's voice have a unique way of igniting memory.** That's because when you hear them, you may remember a specific moment and the way you felt. Did your mom have a favorite band or musician that she enjoyed listening to? Is there a song that you danced to with her? Is there a lullaby she sang to you when you were a young girl? Do you have a voicemail from her? Write down all the ways you can use sound to reminisce.

▶▶▶ **You can create a purposeful connection to your mom by intentionally making contact with things that belonged to her.** Is there a piece of your mom's clothing that you could wear? Can you make a blanket or teddy bear out of some clothing? Is there a special memento that belonged to your mom that you could hold in your hands? Is there a piece of jewelry or watch that you could wear? Make a list of at least five items you can touch to feel a connection to your mom.

▶▶▶ **Aromas can bring up the most personal memories.** Did your mom have a favorite perfume? Was there a candle that she liked to burn? Did your mom cook something special for you that smelled wonderful? Was there a product she used around the house regularly that had a distinct smell? Make a list of five smells you associate with your mom that you can re-create.

▶▶▶ **When we taste something that we have had before, it connects us to memories of special occasions and good times.** What was your mom's favorite meal or snack? Is there a restaurant that she enjoyed? Can you create a new recipe in honor of her? Did she always have a candy or cough drop in her purse to share with you? Make a list of the ways that taste can help you connect to your mom.

It is hard to look closely at the relationship we had with our moms. It may have been beautiful, or it may have been tragic; either way, we reflect on the relationship when grieving. We may want to push our feelings of grief away by avoiding and ignoring them. This is understandable because it is hard to engage with the painful thoughts, feelings, and emotions that surface after our mother dies. I invite you to take a pause and consider the following: Are there emotions you have repressed? Are there feelings that have been bottled up?What have you been sweeping to the side? Confronting the pain of your loss and working through your feelings about your relationship opens up a pathway for recovery. Go deep, look back, and feel all your feelings. Doing so invites restoration and healing.

Recall a Time

Memories are a way to reflect on the entirety of our mother-daughter relationship, and allow us to identify lessons learned and find meaning through the loss. Through an active process of remembering, you can preserve what existed between you and your mother and bring the relationship into the present. This visualization exercise can help you develop a process for actively engaging with memories.

1. Find a quiet comfortable space.

2. Close your eyes, take three deep breaths, and bring forth a memory of your mom.

3. Think about where you were at the time, what was around you, and who you were with.

4. Reflect on the feelings that come up as you think about this memory.

5. Hold the visual picture of this memory in your mind and check in with your body. What sensations are you feeling?

6. Let the movie continue to run in your head. Is there anything you would change or wish was different?

7. Take three deep breaths and open your eyes.

8. Make note of the insight you gained by reviewing this memory. What lessons or meaning come from remembering this experience with your mother?

Remain Curious About Her

You can learn things about your mom, even after she has died. Finding ways to talk about her with family members and friends provides an opportunity for you to ask questions and learn more about her life. What are you curious about? What questions would you ask? Who could you talk with? Write down your questions and who you could talk with about your mom. Set a date and plan a time to get together.

▶▶▶ **We learn about life from our parents, through observing how they have lived their lives; these are called "life lessons."** Moms are known for sharing bits and pieces of knowledge that help us navigate life. What words of wisdom or life lessons have you learned from your mom?

When we reminisce, we are sharing a joyful recollection of past events. These are the times we look back fondly on and enjoy sharing with others. Sharing memories and reminiscing with our girlfriends can be fulfilling. They understand the mother-daughter relationship and can relate to our experiences with our mother. Maybe they knew your mom and have their own experience to share, or maybe they have similar memories of times with their own mother. Either way, engaging in story sharing with a few close friends helps us feel connected to our moms. We can share about either mutual experiences or individual memories of what the past was like. This is shared reminiscence.

▶▶▶ **Family traditions are the way values and culture are transferred from one generation to the next.** They create special bonds that endure over time. You can celebrate your mom's life by continuing her favorite family traditions. Which ones would you like to continue in remembrance of your mom?

▶▶▶ **You've learned about the theory of continuing bonds as a way to understand the relationship that perseveres after our mother dies.** One way is to begin participating in hobbies that your mom enjoyed. Was she a gardener? Did she enjoy arts and crafts? Was she an avid reader? What were some of her hobbies? List three hobbies that your mom enjoyed that you would like to participate in and start one this coming month, even if it's just for one day.

▶▶▶ **When you commit to helping others, you in turn help yourself.** Volunteer with an organization that was important to your mother or offer help to those who are experiencing situations similar to yours right now. It can be a meaningful way to remember your mom. List three potential volunteer opportunities in your community and commit to finding out more about how to volunteer.

What Would Mom Do?

Mothers are known for giving advice. When we are faced with a difficult challenge or have a problem we need to solve, we can find ourselves missing our moms and looking for her wisdom. As daughters, our mothers are role models for us—in both positive and negative ways. We admired our moms and want to emulate her, or we despised something that she did and would never want to repeat it. In the table below, write four things your mom did that you would like to continue doing and four things your mom did that you would never do. Use this as a guide for how you will remain connected to the wisdom your mom shared.

What you'd like to continue doing:	What you'll likely never do:

►►► **New rituals provide an opportunity for family to remember and share in their grief.** For example, say your mom loved pink roses; you could start a tradition of having a single pink rose at every family gathering. Brainstorm three new family rituals that you can create in honor of your mom.

▶▶▶ **Our values serve as a road map for our lives.** Core values, the deepest and most valuable qualities we hope to guide our lives by, can be linked back to our mom through observations of how she lived her life, even if we didn't agree with some of her choices. Think about the values that were important to your mother. How did they shape her life? How do those core values influence you today?

▶▶▶**Designating a dedicated space as a memorial or shrine in your home can assist with regulating your emotions and facilitating a positive connection to your mom.** Consider creating a space outdoors in a garden or find a shelf inside your home where you can place memorial items. Use the space below to write about some ideas for creating a memorial space. Include potential items and locations.

▶▶▶ **Creative expression helps us express our deeper feelings of grief about the loss of our mother, especially the feelings that we may be struggling to find words for.** Imagine you were able to visualize your grief. What would it look like? What images begin to surface? Think about different colors and shapes, and whatever else comes to mind. Draw a picture of what your grief feels like.

▶▶▶ **Finding ways to talk about your mom is a great way to keep your relationship present.** Whether it is sharing memories with friends or family members or talking about your mom with co-workers or new acquaintances, when you share it keeps her in your present mind, in present time. If you were to introduce your mom to a new acquaintance, what would you say? Use the space below to write your introduction.

Write a Tribute to Your Mom

Imagine that you have been asked to make a presentation to a group of people who have never met your mom. In your tribute speech, you should recall favorite memories, reflect on the significance of your mother in your life, and talk about her personality and what made her unique. As you write, examine your heart and take a trip down memory lane. Say what is important to say and share about the pain of your loss. Use this exercise to connect with your mother and allow yourself to acknowledge her presence and legacy.

▶▶▶ **As daughters, we want to make our moms proud of us.** We seek their approval in different ways, and when we live our lives in a way that makes them proud, it facilitates a strong connection. In what ways do you believe that you make your mom proud?

"There are no goodbyes for us . . . Wherever you are, you will always be in my heart." —MAHATMA GANDHI

"The highest tribute to the dead
is not grief but gratitude."

—THORNTON WILDER, *OUR TOWN*

5

USING GRATITUDE TO GRIEVE

———

Gratitude can be defined as "a strong feeling of appreciation for someone or for what that person has done for you." Intentionally engaging in gratitude as part of your grieving process puts you on a path back to happiness and helps you recover from this loss with strength. Even if you didn't have a great relationship with your mother or perhaps had no relationship at all, focusing on gratitude allows you to invest in what you do have in other meaningful relationships. When you think about your mom, let the memories of her take hold in a way that you can appreciate and cherish; remember to value that she gave birth to you and the role she played in your life. In this section, you will use journal prompts, reflections, and exercises to cultivate a sense of gratitude to heal from the loss of your mother.

Leaning into gratitude means that you are actively connecting to what you are thankful for. At first it can be hard to focus on gratitude when you're grieving. But when you make space for the small things you're grateful for and begin to verbalize how you feel, those feelings of despair will shift to feelings of joy. It will not happen overnight, so a commitment to expressing gratitude as a regular practice is important here. Learning to identify the things that mean the most to you and focus on the beauty of the life that your mom gave you is an important part of your journey.

▶▶▶ **Gratitude starts with giving thanks. List a few things you are thankful to have experienced with your mom.** It could be a favorite birthday party, a special meal on a special night, family gatherings, bedtime stories, or a hug when you needed one. Find what is meaningful to you.

Write a Letter of Gratitude

This exercise is an opportunity for you to offer thanks to your mom for something she did or said. Think of this as a letter of appreciation, and a powerful way to build strength and foster resilience as you grieve the loss of your mom.

Set aside 30 minutes and find a comfortable space to do your writing. Begin by thinking about three things that your mom has done that you are grateful for and the impact that those things have had on your life. Describe those things in detail; picture them in your mind and write about the images as you recall them. Reflect on how those things have shaped you and made you who you are today. Thank your mom for what she gave you and how that helps you now.

▶▶▶ **We grow through our experiences, both the good and the bad.** I am sure there were many times when you were happy about the way things turned out or sad about a failed attempt at something. Write about one experience you had with your mom that shaped the woman you are today.

▶▶▶ **We are introduced to the world through our mom.** She may have talked about a place with enthusiasm or shared stories about her travels; maybe you even had an opportunity to travel with her. Write about a place you feel grateful to have traveled to, whom you traveled with, and why.

Expressing gratitude doesn't come easy for many. A daily practice of fostering gratitude will bring comfort to your grieving process. Over time you will find that you can look back at your relationship with your mom with gladness. Get started by remembering the small things that your mom did for you, such as how she phoned to check in on you or the way she always made your favorite dessert. Make it a daily practice to remember one thing that you can give thanks to your mom for, even if your choices are limited. Focus on this handful of things.

Collecting Daily Moments of Gratitude

For this exercise, you're going test out the theory of an everyday practice of gratitude. Find a decorative glass jar, container, or box and place it somewhere you will see each day. Each morning for 30 days, write something you are grateful for on a slip of paper. Examples include a warm cup of morning tea, a thoughtful text from a friend, or a memory of your mom. Put the piece of paper into the gratitude container and keep adding to the collection each day. As the container fills up and becomes full, it signals that there are things to be hopeful about and that there are good things in the world. It helps shift our mindset from what we have lost to all that we have gained. Once the gratitude container is full, empty it and read the slips of paper. Rereading all those words of appreciation will lift your spirits and bring a smile to your face as you reflect on these small moments of gratitude.

▶▶▶ **Preserving memories of times we shared with our mother is an important part of our grieving process.** Our memories serve to keep us connected to our mom and allow us to be thankful for what we had. What is a memory of your mom that you are grateful for having? How has it helped you?

▶▶▶ **We receive support and comfort from others as we grieve, sometimes in the most unexpected ways.** Write about a good experience that you are grateful for having while grieving the loss of your mom.

Expressing gratitude while grieving the loss of your mother is about proactively celebrating all the wonderful relationships you have in your life. This act is one of the most positive coping strategies that you can employ in your grief. When you express appreciation for others and yourself on a daily basis, it makes you feel good, and makes others feel good too. With gratitude you become more optimistic, your relationships flourish, and you experience greater satisfaction with life. Let gratitude become part of your healing path. Begin today.

▶▶▶ **Leaning on others and accepting help when grieving give us strength.**
Help may come from someone close or just a friendly face in the neighborhood
like the cashier at the grocery store or the barista at your favorite coffee shop.
Who are the people who have been most helpful as you adapt to living in a
world without your mom? Write their names here and how their support has
eased your grief.

▶▶▶ **When we are grieving the loss of our mom, we encounter moments of sadness.** At these times, a moment of kindness from a friend or a simple caring act from a co-worker can shift our mood. Write about something someone did recently to cheer you up when you were feeling down.

Give Hope to Your Future Self

In this exercise, you will be writing a letter to your future self. The goals of writing this letter are to gain perspective about this loss in your life and instill hope for the future. Set aside 30 minutes for this exercise and find a comfortable space to write.

Begin by thinking about 10 years into the future. What do want to remember from this time of grief? What has been your experience so far? What have you learned about grief? Who or what has helped? Reflect on this moment in time and the gains you have experienced. What are you grateful for? What or who is most important? What current challenges are you facing and what have you learned from them?

Define your hopes for your future self. What will your life be like? Think about family, friends, and other relationships. How will this loss become integrated into your life? Reflect on what your grief will feel like in 10 years. What else do you wish for yourself? Once you are done, put the letter in a safe place to be retrieved at a future point in time.

▶▶▶ **Gratitude should be expressed toward others and toward ourselves.**
Think about a time when you were younger, when you did something that you
have appreciation for. Show gratitude toward your younger self and write about
one thing you are proud of yourself for doing and why.

....

....

....

....

Now express the same gratitude for someone else. Write about someone who is
special to you and why.

....

....

....

....

....

....

....

▶▶ **Family traditions connect to history and create lasting legacy.** They become important touchstones for memories and reflections of past times. Write about five family traditions that you are grateful for and why they bring you happiness.

Let's take a moment to think about lessons you have learned from your past. Taking time to remember these moments and feel grateful for the memories can help you in your grief journey, because they remind you that you can grow from your experiences. What major life lesson do you feel most grateful for learning?

A Gratitude Meditation

Meditation provides an opportunity for us to contemplate our thoughts on a particular topic. In this case, we are exploring gratitude. When we focus on gratitude, it connects us to positive emotions and shifts attention from what we don't have to what we do have. Use this mediation to explore feelings of gratitude for the important people in your life today.

1. Sit in a comfortable position and close your eyes.

2. Take three breaths, inhaling and exhaling for a count of three on each breath.

3. Bring your attention to your chest and heart. Take three breaths.

4. Think about someone that you are grateful for. Take three breaths.

5. Focus on feelings of love, kindness, and appreciation for this person. Continue breathing.

6. Allow your heart to connect to the joy and beauty of their presence in your life. Take three breaths.

7. Reflect on the gratitude you feel in your body. Pause. Take three breaths.

8. Open your eyes and express gratitude to yourself for completing this meditation.

9. Use the space below to make note of the gratitude you are feeling right now.

▶▶▶ **Mothers are considered role models and can be one of the most influential figures in our lives, although they may not be the only person who has influences on us.** Write about someone you admire and the positive impact they have had on you.

▶▶▶ **Following the loss of your mother, your outlook for the future can be bleak.** Anticipating positive things helps us look forward with gratitude. Write about five things you hope will happen in the next year.

"But behind all your stories is always your mother's story, because hers is where yours begins."
—MITCH ALBOM, *FOR ONE MORE DAY*

"Goodbyes are only for those who love with their eyes. Because for those who love with heart and soul there is no such thing as separation."

—RUMI, *MASNAVI*

6

MOVING ON WITHOUT LETTING GO

It's hard to believe that we experience growth as a result of our loss, but we do. Grieving the loss of your mother never ends; you simply learn how to live with it. The demands of grief lessen, and the severity of it diminishes. Our identity as a daughter changes as we discover new ways of connecting to the world without our mother. Life continues forward as new possibilities are discovered and new dreams are created. Happiness returns. Our families change and so do we as individuals. As life takes on new purpose and meaning, you still have permission to grieve the loss of your mother, no matter how much time has passed. Grief remains a silent partner at the ready. You will need space for grief, even years after your mother's death. This section will provide you with exercises, prompts, and reflections to assist with creating meaning as you continue to heal and move forward.

Grief is a long, winding road. You will learn how to navigate all the twists, turns, and curves on the road as you grieve the loss of your mother. You will also grieve the experience of having a mother. There will no longer be anyone to fulfill the role of mother in your life and your role as a daughter will be different. You will grieve acutely at first and the intensity of grief will subside as you become accustomed to living in a world without your mom. This is not an easy process, but you will find a way through grief. Grief will be a catalyst for growth as you begin to live with this loss. Your life will be forever changed, but your mother will always live on through you.

Letting Go of Past Regrets

Fully healing from this loss means that you can let go of grief because there is a lasting connection to your mom in other ways. To truly let go of your grief, you will need to get rid of any remaining painful feelings or regrets. Holding on to these negative feelings and regrets keeps you anchored in the past. Use this exercise to let go of any remaining bad feelings or regrets that you are holding on to.

1. On a piece of paper, write down all the bad feelings and regrets that you continue to have about your mom and her death. Make sure to include any long-standing regrets that you are holding. *Example: I feel terrible about not spending more time with my mom in her final weeks. I wish that I were a less rebellious teenager and made life easier for my mom.*

2. Review your list and gather any items that remind you of those hurtful or painful situations, events, or feelings. Examples could include pictures, emails, a piece of clothing, or other items.

3. Place the paper and any items you have gathered in a container.

4. Take your container filled with past regrets and release them by disposing of the contents in the container.

5. Congratulate yourself for releasing these regrets and remind yourself that letting go of them is healing.

6. Use the space below to write about how it feels to release these regrets and move forward unburdened.

▶▶▶ **Experiencing joy following the loss of your mother can be unfathomable.**
However, it is important to recognize simple pleasures as a good place to start.
List five simple pleasures you have experienced in the last week.

▶▶▶**Thinking that we can be truly happy again can feel impossible.** Although you are no longer able to experience happiness with your mom, you can derive happiness in other ways. Write about five things that make you happy now.

▶▶▶**Laughter is healing.** When you laugh, you release stress and tension. Laughter connects us to fun, joyful memories. Find humor in the memories of good times you had with your mom. Write about a memory that is connected to your mother that makes you laugh.

The calendar changes after your mom dies. You now have your own private grief calendar that includes her death anniversary and the day you were informed she was going to die or had died. We navigate around these painful days and they become touch points for our grief. Let your private grief calendar serve as a reminder to strengthen bonds with those you love and share in the joy of living to honor your mom.

Planning for Significant Days

Holidays such as Thanksgiving, birthdays, and Mother's Day can be triggers for grief. Other days that were significant to both you and your mom can also inspire grief. These days can take you by surprise if you don't plan for them. Making a plan to navigate these days can reduce feelings of grief and bring a sense of peace and connectedness to those days. Select two to three items from this list to add to your calendar as activities that you can participate in on significant days.

1. Help others on special days, or assist those who are experiencing situations similar to what you have experienced.

2. Donate in your mom's name. Purchase a book and donate it to your local library or school. Be sure to place a label inside the front cover inscribed, "In memory of . . ."

3. On birthdays, anniversaries, or holidays, buy your mom a gift and then donate it to a hospital, nursing home, or other care facility.

4. Select a greeting card that you wish your mom would have picked for you, and mail it to yourself.

5. Give yourself a gift from your mom that you always wished she had given you, and think of her whenever you use it or wear it.

▶▶▶ **The grief we feel for our mom will reemerge at different times.** Some of these moments are unexpected and others can be predicted. Getting married, having a child, or achieving a career or education goal are examples of future events that may trigger grief. Think about future events that will be difficult for you and create a plan for how you can manage grief during those times. Write about the coping strategies and support systems that have helped you thus far and how they might help in the future.

Your Future You

Envisioning a picture for your future self creates a sense of purpose. Having goals for the future helps ground you as you continue to move through grief. What are your short-term goals for the next four months? What about the next two years?

▶▶▶ **Grief changes throughout our lifetime.** No matter how much we grieve immediately following the loss of our mom, that grief will show up again at significant milestones in our lives. Grief changes, and we change too. In what ways has your grief changed you?

As we emerge from the depths of grief, we become more hopeful about the future and reengage in our life in new and meaningful ways. There are rituals that generate life, which can symbolize hope, define purpose, and create meaning. Consider planting a tree, bush, shrub, flower bed or garden as a long-lasting, living memorial to your mom that will grow over time. It's okay to keep loving your mom after she dies. Love doesn't die; it continues to grow inside us, even after death. Let your love grow.

▶▶▶ **Connecting with other daughters who have lost their mothers will help you discover new ways to cope along with others who are able to understand and relate to your experience.** You can join a local support group or become a member of an online community. What steps can you take to connect with other daughters who are grieving?

Write Your Grief Story

You are going to write a story about your grief. It doesn't need to be more than a few paragraphs, but it should begin with the sentence, "When my mother died . . ."

Start there and let your thoughts and feelings flow. Allow yourself the freedom to say all the things that you have been holding inside. As you write, examine your heart and connect to what is broken and what is joyful. Say what is important to say and share about the pain of your loss. Use this exercise to connect with your innermost feelings about the loss of your mother and your grief.

_____

_____

_____

_____

_____

_____

_____

_____

_____

_____

Grief rituals are restorative activities that provide a road map for interacting with our grief. Engaging in these rituals on days when your heart is heavy will give you the needed space to grieve. Add to these rituals over time and commit to nurturing yourself regularly. You will have difficult days when you miss your mom, crave her touch, and need her advice. This is normal. Grief rituals are a form of self-care. They quickly release painful emotions and unpleasant recollections, allowing your positive memories to come forward and restore a sense of well-being. Nurture yourself.

Growing through Grief

"Post-traumatic growth" refers to positive psychological change experienced as a result of adversity. This was researched by psychologists Richard G. Tedeschi and Lawrence G. Calhoun at the University of North Carolina at Charlotte. Growth does not occur as a direct result of trauma; rather, it is the individual's struggle with their new reality in the aftermath of loss or trauma. In what ways have you grown in the aftermath of the loss of your mother?

▶▶▶ **We sometimes uncover strengths that we never knew existed after the loss of someone close to us.** Think about the loss of your mother and the ways that you are stronger because of this experience. Do you worry less? Are you better able to persevere? Can you bounce back more quickly when things don't go as planned?

▶▶▶ **Only you can find meaning in the loss of your mother. Nobody else can tell you what that is or how to make sense of what has happened.** Maybe you feel a renewed or greater appreciation for life or see new possibilities for yourself. When we find meaning in our loss, it gives purpose to our pain. What do you see as the true purpose of this loss?

It is expected that you will experience waves of intense grief even years after your mom's death. Over the years, you will develop a greater awareness of triggers and be more skilled at managing grief. New family traditions will form over time and new ways to connect to your mom will emerge. Life will be different, but it can be just as good.

▶▶▶ **As you move through grief, you face many things with which you'll have to contend, but most of all you will find ways to take care of yourself.** What have you learned about caring for yourself because of this loss?

▶▶▶ **Grief teaches us about the world and ourselves.** We discover new and interesting things about others and our appreciation for life can increase. What have you learned—about community, about people, about human nature—because of the loss of your mother?

What advice would you give to other daughters who are living with the loss of their mother?

"People die, I think, but your relationship with them doesn't. It continues and is ever-changing."
—JANDY NELSON, *I'LL GIVE YOU THE SUN*

Resources

WEBSITES:

Modern Loss (ModernLoss.com)

Option B (OptionB.org)

What's Your Grief? (WhatsYourGrief.com)

BOOKS:

The Body Keeps the Score: Brain, Mind, and Body in the Healing of Trauma by Bessel van der Kolk, MD

Grief Is a Journey: Finding Your Path through Loss by Dr. Kenneth J. Doka

Liberating Losses: When Death Brings Relief by Jennifer Elison, EdD and Chris McGonigle, PhD

The Mindbody Prescription: Healing the Body, Healing the Pain by John E. Sarno, MD

Motherless Daughters: The Legacy of Loss by Hope Edelman

Wild: From Lost to Found on the Pacific Crest Trail by Cheryl Strayed

OTHER JOURNALS:

Healing After Loss: Daily Meditations for Working through Grief by Martha Whitmore Hickman

Progressing Through Grief: Guided Exercises to Understand Your Emotions and Recover from Loss by Stephanie Jose

Your Grief, Your Way: A Year of Practical Guidance and Comfort After Loss by Shelby Forsythia

References

Bowlby, John. *Loss: Sadness and Depression, Volume III.* New York: Basic Books, 1982.

Humphrey, Keren M. *Counseling Strategies for Loss and Grief.* Alexandria, VA: The American Counseling Association, 2009.

Jeffreys, J. Shep. *Helping Grieving People: When Tears Are Not Enough.* New York: Routledge, 2011.

Klass, Dennis, Phyllis R. Silverman, and Steven L. Nickman, eds. *Continuing Bonds: New Understandings of Grief.* New York: Taylor & Francis, 1996.

Kübler-Ross, Elisabeth. *On Death and Dying: What the Dying Have to Teach Doctors, Nurses, Clergy & Their Own Families.* New York: Macmillian, 1969.

Lambert, Nathaniel M., Steven M. Graham, Frank D. Fincham, and Tyler F. Stillman. "A Changed Perspective: How Gratitude Can Affect Sense of Coherence through Positive Reframing." *The Journal of Positive Psychology* 4, no. 6 (November 2009): 461–470. doi: 10.1080 /17439760903157182.

Lewis, C. S. *A Grief Observed.* New York: HarperCollins Publishers, 1969.

Muratori, Michelle, and Robert Haynes. *Coping Skills for a Stressful World: A Workbook for Counselors and Clients.* Alexandria, VA: The American Counseling Association, 2020.

Neimeyer, Robert A., Darcy L. Harris, Howard R. Winokuer, and Gordon F. Thornton, eds. *Grief and Bereavement in Contemporary Society.* New York: Routledge, 2011.

Neimeyer, Robert A., ed. *Techniques of Grief Therapy.* New York: Routledge, 2016.

Rando, Therese A. *How to Go On Living When Someone You Love Dies.* New York: Bantam, 1991.

Stroebe, M., and Schut, H. "The Dual Process Model of Coping with Bereavement: Rationale and Description." *Death Studies* 23, no. 3 (1999): 197–224.

Volkan, Vamik D. *Linking Objects and Linking Phenomena: A Study of the Forms, Symptoms, Metapsychology, and Therapy of Complicated Mourning.* New York: International University Press, 1981.

Worden, William J. *Grief Counseling and Grief Therapy: A Handbook for the Mental Health Practitioner.* New York: Springer Publishing Company, 2008.

Acknowledgments

My personal journey with grief began in 1993 following the unfathomable loss of my father and again in 1996 with the loss of my brother, John. It is through these losses that I developed an interest in understanding grief. Thank you, Dad. Thank you, John. I am eternally grateful for all the lessons you have taught me over the years, both in life and after.

This book would not have been possible without the love and support of my family and friends. I want to thank them for always encouraging me to explore my interests and live life to the fullest.

And, to my love, Mark, who always supports my endeavors and lifts my spirits when I need encouragement. Life is better with you by my side.

About the Author

 **Diane P. Brennan** is a licensed mental health counselor specializing in grief and loss. She has been in private practice in New York City since 2015. In 2018, she founded The 20-20 Grief Project to focus on talking with people about their losses from more than 20 years ago. This is a project of shared human connectedness, vulnerability, and kindness for those sharing and listening to these stories of pain and loss.

CPSIA information can be obtained
at www.ICGtesting.com
Printed in the USA
BVHW060123240122
626967BV00002B/2

9 781638 070580